RL: 3.1
PTS: 1/2

DATE DUE

	SEP 21		
MAR 11	SEP 29		
SEP 22	OCT 27		
	JAN 26		
SEP 30			
NOV 04	MAR 07		
NOV 11			
	APR 25		
DEC 01	DEC 06		
DEC 08			
DEC 15			
JAN 19			
MAR 03			
SEP 14			

Demco, Inc. 38-293

A Baby Lobster Grows Up

by Katie Marsico

Children's Press®
A Division of Scholastic Inc.
New York Toronto London Auckland Sydney
Mexico City New Delhi Hong Kong
Danbury, Connecticut

These content vocabulary word builders are for grades 1–2.

Subject Consultant: Susan H. Gray, MS, Zoology

Reading Consultant: Cecilia Minden-Cupp, PhD, Former Director of the Language and Literacy Program, Harvard Graduate School of Education, Cambridge, Massachusetts

Photographs © 2007: Alamy Images: cover left inset, 5 bottom right, 10, 20 bottom (Roland Birke/PHOTOTAKE Inc.), cover center inset, 5 top right, 8 (Alistair Dove), 23 top left (Juniors Bildarchiv), 9, 20 top left (Colin Shepherd); Alistair Dove: back cover, 4 bottom right, 6, 20 center left; Corbis Images: 2, 4 top, 19, 20 right, 21 left (Brownie Harris), 11 (Bruce Robison), 15 top, 21 bottom, 23 bottom right (Jeffrey L. Rotman); NHPA/Anthony Bannister: 16, 21 top; Norbert Wu Photography: 5 bottom left, 15 bottom; Photo Researchers, NY: cover right inset, 1, 7 (Andrew J. Martinez), 5 top left, 23 top right (Tom McHugh), 23 bottom left (Mark Smith); Seapics. com: 17 (Andrew J. Martinez), cover background, 4 bottom left, 13, 21 center right (Espen Rekdal).

Book Design: Simonsays Design!
Book Production: The Design Lab

Library of Congress Cataloging-in-Publication Data
Marsico, Katie, 1980–
A baby lobster grows up / by Katie Marsico.
    p. cm. — (Scholastic news nonfiction readers)
Includes bibliographical references and index.
ISBN-13: 978-0-531-17475-3
ISBN-10: 0-531-17475-1
1. Lobsters—Development—Juvenile literature. I. Title. II. Series.
QL444.M33M3374 2007
595.3'84—dc22   2006025604

1 2 3 4 5 6 7 8 9 10 R 16 15 14 13 12 11 10 09 08 07

CONTENTS

WORD HUNT

Look for these words as you read. They will be in **bold**.

adult
(**ah**-duhlt)

juvenile
(**joo**-vuh-nile)

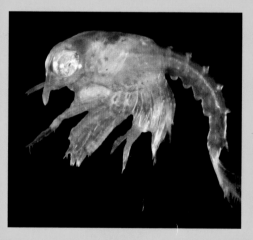

larva
(**lar**-vuh)

4

crustaceans
(kruss-**tay**-shuhnz)

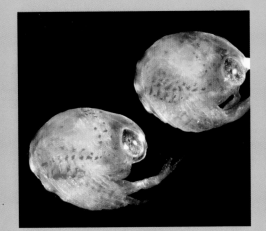

hatch
(hach)

molting
(**molt**-ing)

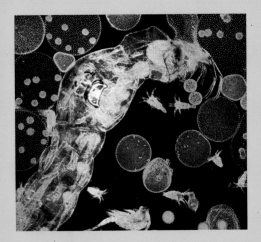

plankton
(**plang**-tuhn)

Baby Lobsters!

What's that tiny animal floating through the water? It is a baby lobster! A baby lobster is called a **larva**.

Lobsters are **crustaceans**. A crustacean's skeleton is outside its body.

How does a lobster grow?

lobster larva

Crustaceans have many legs and four feelers.

A mother lobster lays thousands of eggs.

The eggs stay attached to the bottom of her tail for nine to twelve months.

Finally, the eggs float away. The larvae **hatch**, or come out of their eggs.

larva
hatching

Look at all the tiny, black eggs on this lobster's tail!

A lobster larva floats near the top of the water.

It drifts along with a group of other tiny plants and animals. Together, this group of tiny living things is called **plankton**.

Life is dangerous for lobster larvae. Birds and fish hunt them.

plankton

Some people say a tiny lobster larva looks like a bug. What do you think?

About fifteen to thirty days after a larva hatches, it becomes a better swimmer.

The larva begins to swim up and down in the water. It is looking for a place to settle.

Soon, the larva will settle on the ocean floor. This is where the larva will spend the rest of its life.

A young lobster rests on a sea star.

13

The hard covering, or shell, of a lobster larva doesn't grow with the lobster. As the larva gets bigger, it sheds its shell. This is called **molting**. After molting, a new shell hardens over the larva to protect it.

A larva looks more like a grown-up lobster each time it molts.

Did you know that grown-up lobsters molt, too?

A two-month-old larva after molting.

An adult lobster molts.

15

A **juvenile** lobster keeps molting and growing.

After a while, it learns to hunt fish, clams, and sea urchins.

sea urchins

Lobsters often hide in seaweed or between rocks.

A lobster becomes an **adult** at about five to seven years old. You can guess how old a lobster is by its size. Lobsters get bigger as they get older.

The largest lobster ever caught weighed 44 pounds (20 kilograms). Some people think that lobster might have been 100 years old!

A lobster climbs over a rock on the ocean floor.

A BABY LOBSTER GROWS UP!

1 A mother lobster lays thousands of eggs.

2 The eggs hatch nine to twelve months later. Out come the larvae!

3 A lobster larva floats near the top of the water with plankton.

7 All grown up!
A lobster becomes
an adult when it
is five to seven
years old.

6 Hungry juvenile
lobsters learn to
hunt clams, fish,
and sea urchins.

5 After about
fifteen to thirty
days, the larvae
begin to swim
toward the ocean floor.

4 The larva molts
as it grows.

YOUR NEW WORDS

adult (**ah**-duhlt) a grown-up person or animal

crustaceans (kruss-**tay**-shuhnz) animals with outer skeletons, many legs, and four feelers

hatch (hach) to break out of an egg

juvenile (**joo**-vuh-nile) a young person or animal

larva (**lar**-vuh) a baby lobster that has just hatched from its egg; two or more babies are called larvae

molting (**molt**-ing) shedding skin

plankton (**plang**-tuhn) a group of tiny plants and animals that float together in the water

THESE ANIMALS ARE CRUSTACEANS, TOO!

crab

crayfish

pill bug

shrimp

INDEX

FIND OUT MORE

Book:

Rake, Jody Sullivan. *Lobsters*. Mankato, Minn.: Pebble Books, 2007.

Website:

The Lobster Institute: Kids' Page
http://www.lobster.um.maine.edu/index.php?page=18

MEET THE AUTHOR

Katie Marsico lives with her family outside of Chicago, Illinois. She learned a lot about lobsters while writing this book. She and her husband, Carl, think lobsters are too cute to eat!